I0005355

Android 6 Programming

Android Studio Development Guide

By Mark Smart

Copyright©2016 by Mark Smart

All Rights Reserved

Copyright © 2016 by Mark Smart

All rights reserved. No part of this publication may be reproduced, distributed, or transmitted in any form or by any means, including photocopying, recording, or other electronic or mechanical methods, without the prior written permission of the author, except in the case of brief quotations embodied in critical reviews and certain other noncommercial uses permitted by copyright law.

Table of Contents

Disclaimer

While all attempts have been made to verify the information provided in this book, the author does assume any responsibility for errors, omissions, or contrary interpretations of the subject matter contained within. The information provided in this book is for educational and entertainment purposes only. The reader is responsible for his or her own actions and the author does not accept any responsibilities for any liabilities or damages, real or perceived, resulting from the use of this information.

The trademarks that are used are without any consent, and the publication of the trademark is without permission or backing by the trademark owner. All trademarks and brands within this book are for clarifying purposes only and are the owned by the owners themselves, not affiliated with this document. **

Introduction

Recently, the Android development team released the 6th version of Android Studio. This has a number of features which help Android software developers to create their apps easily and quickly. The process of creating the user interface for Android apps has become much easier. The IDE is open source, so you can download and use it for free and begin to develop your Android apps.

Chapter 1- The Code Editor in Android 6

Whenever you are creating an Android app, you do a lot of coding, and you have to check your code and correct any mistakes which may arise. It has been found that most Android developers spend most of their time while editing their code to make it correct. This is usually done within the editor window.

With the modern code editor in Android Studio 6, the Code Editor has been advanced beyond typing, copying, pasting, and deleting of the code. The effectiveness of a code editor for any programming language is gauged by determining how much it makes it easy for us to navigate through the code of the app, how effective it is in terms of detecting and highlighting the errors in our code, and the amount it reduces the amount that we are expected to type in the editor.

The Android Studio's code editor has been created to help Android developers write their code easily. Most of its functionalities are similar to those of the other text editors, but there are some areas in which it excels.

Whenever you select some code for editing, may it be XML, Java, or any other text; the code editor will be displayed at the center of the window. Consider the code editor given below, having a Java Source code:

```
package com.ebookfrenzy.androidsample;

import ...

public class AndroidSampleActivity extends AppCompatActivity {

    @Override
    protected void onCreate(Bundles savedInstanceState) {
        super.onCreate(savedInstanceState);
        setContentView(R.layout.activity android sample);
```

The code editor is made up of the following elements:

Document Tabs

With Android Studio, multiple files can be opened for editing at the same time. Since you have opened multiple files, each is displayed in its tab, and the name of each file is displayed on its tab at the top bar.

Sometimes, it becomes impossible for all of the tabs to be displayed on the window. In such a case, you will observe a drop-down menu at the right corner of the window. If you click on the menu, additional files which are open will be shown. If you observe a wavy red line under the name of the file in its tab, just know that there is some code in the file which has one or more errors.

For you to switch between the tabs, you have to click on each respective tab or use the Alt-Left and Alt-Right keys. For you to be able to run the code in a file, all the errors have to be corrected. Otherwise, you will get an error. The switcher mechanism can also be used for the purpose of alternating between the files opened in the code editor.

The Editor Gutter Area

This area is used by the editor for the purpose of displaying icons and controls. Examples of controls which can be found in this area include the controls for folding and unfolding blocks of code, debugging breakpoint markers, line numbers, change markers, and bookmarks. The default setting is that the line numbers are hidden, but you can still enable them by right clicking on the gutter area and then choosing the option for "Show Line Numbers menu."

The Status Bar

Although the status bar may be viewed as only part of the main window, it plays a great role in the code editor. It carries some information regarding the editing session which is currently active. It provides us with information regarding the current cursor position in terms of characters and lines and the format of encoding used in the file. If you click on these on the status bar, it will be possible for you to change these. An example is that when you click on the line number, the Go to Line dialog will be displayed.

Editor Area

This represents the area in which your code is to be displayed. You have to enter it here and then edit it.

Validation and Marker Sidebar

A feature named "on-the-fly code analysis" was introduced in Android Studio. This feature just means that during the process of typing the code, the editor will be doing an analysis to check for any errors and warnings in the code. This will be shown by changes in the color of the indicator located at the top of your validation sidebar. The color will always change between red, yellow, and green. If you click on the indicator, you will view information regarding the types of errors and other issues which have been found in the code written in the cod editor.

If some errors are found in your code, the sidebar will also show marks at the places where these errors are found. If the line with the error is visible and then you hover the mouse pointer over the marker, a description of the error will be shown.

How to Split the Editor Window

The default setting is that the code editor will show the code of the selected file in the window. However, not all times will you be working with a single source file, as there are times when you will be working with different source files simultaneously. In such a situation, you will need to display them on the editor in panels, meaning that these have to be split. If you need to split the editor, just right click on the tab for the file and then choose to split it either vertically or horizontally, depending on how you want the panels to appear.

The window shown below shows an editor being split into three panels:

However, it is possible for you to change how the split panels have been oriented at any time. You just have to right click the corresponding tab, and then select the option for *"Change Splitter Orientation menu."* If you need to unsplit a single panel, you just have to follow the same steps, but this time around, you have to split the option for *"unsplit"* menu from the presented options. To unsplit all the panels, you have to select the option for unsplit all from the menu option.

Window splitting is very good when we need to display different files, or when we need to have multiple windows in a single file, and this will make it possible for us to view the different parts of a file at the same time and perform the necessary editing.

Code Completion

The Code editor in Android Studio comes with built-in knowledge about the syntax used in java programming language, together with the methods and other properties of the language. The Studio is also aware of the code base we use and the method found in the Android SDK. As you type your code, the editor makes a reference to know what you may need, and suggests for you what you may need so as to complete the statement instead of having to type the whole statement. Most people know this feature as auto-completion, which is still okay. Once the editor has found some suggestions regarding whatever you might be typing, a panel will be presented to you with numerous options for the suggestions.

Consider the example figure given below, which shows how suggestions are presented to the user:

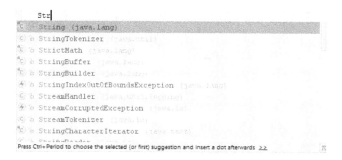

In case you don't find any appropriate suggestion from the ones provided, it will be good for you to continue typing your statement. If more proper suggestions are found, they will be presented to you and then choose them. However, if you find them early in advance, just select the right choice from the provided suggestions.

If you need to invoke the suggestions manually when typing, just hit a ctrl-space keyboard sequence. If you need to replace the word you have typed with the one highlighted in the suggestion box, just press the tab key.

Other than the auto-completion feature in Android Studio, another feature referred to as Smart Completion is also offered. For you to invoke this, you have to use the key sequence of Shift-Ctrl-Space, and if you select it, you will be provided with several suggestions depending on the context of your current code. This one provides you with a wide range of suggestions from which you can choose.

When it comes to different programmers, code completion is just a choice, as some people like it, while others do not like it. There are some people who need to summarize the codes or memorize them so that they can easily remember them. In the case of such individuals, then completion will not be good for you. However, in the case of the rest of the individuals, if you are in a hurry, just use the completion feature, and you will create your apps quickly.

Statement Completion

Statement completion is also another form of auto completion which is provided in Android Studio. This is a form of auto completion which is normally used for the purpose of completing the brackets for methods, functions, and other properties of your Android code. To invoke the feature statement completion in Android Studio, you have to press the keys Shift-Ctrl-Enter.

Consider the example code given below:

protected void method()

Once you have typed the above code into the editor, and then invoked the statement completion, the brackets will automatically be filled so that you have something which looks as shown below:

```
protected void method() {


}
```

Parameter Information

In Android Studio, it is possible for one to ask about the parameter arguments which are accepted by a particular method. Once the cursor has been positioned between the brackets of your method call, just hit a Ctrl-P key sequence and this will display for you the parameters which the method is expected to accept. Note that the suggestion which is seen to be the likely one will be highlighted in bold.

Code Generation

Rather than generating some code as it is being typed on the editor, it is possible for us to generate the whole code. To show the list of options which can be used for generating the code, you can use the key combination of Alt-Insert. However, make sure that you have the cursor in the file in which you need to generate the code. These are shown below:

Generate

Constructor

Getter

Setter

Getter and Setter

equals() and hashCode()

toString()

Override Methods...

Delegate Methods...

Copyright

To demonstrate this using an example, consider an example in which you need to be notified by the system once your code is almost being destroyed by the operating system. For us to implement this, we have to override the onStop() lifecycle method in the activity of our superclass. For us to generate a stub method of this in Android Studio, you have to select the option "override methods" from the generation list of your code and then select the *"onStop()"* method. This will be among the list of the methods which will be displayed.

```
m  🔓 ActionBarActivity()
m  🔓 getSupportActionBar():ActionBar
m  🔓 getMenuInflater():MenuInflater
m  🔓 setContentView(layoutResID:int):void
m  🔓 setContentView(view:View):void
m  🔓 setContentView(view:View, params:LayoutParam
m  🔓 addContentView(view:View, params:LayoutParan
m  🔓 onConfigurationChanged(newConfig:Configurat
m  🔑 onStop():void
m  🔑 onPostResume():void
m  🔓 onCreatePanelView(featureId:int):View
m  🔑 onTitleChanged(title:CharSequence, color:int):vo
m  🔓 supportRequestWindowFeature(featureId:int):bo(
m  🔓 supportInvalidateOptionsMenu():void
m  🔓 onSupportActionModeStarted(mode:ActionMod
m  🔓 onSupportActionModeFinished(mode:ActionMo
m  🔓 startSupportActionMode(callback:Callback):Actic
m  🔓 onCreatePanelMenu(featureId:int, menu:Menu):t
m  🔓 onPreparePanel(featureId:int, view:View, menu:N
```

Now that you have selected the method which you need to override, just click on the ok button which will then stub method for you at the current location of your cursor in the Java file. This is shown in the code given below:

```
@Override
protected void onStop() {
    super.onStop();
}
```

Code Folding

Once a file with the source code has reached a certain size, it may become difficult for us to manage or navigate through the code, despite how well it might been organized or formatted. Android Studio will always take the view of the content in which it is not a must for us to have the content block code visible at all times. For us to navigate easily via the code in Android Studio's code editor, we can use the code folding feature. For us to control code folding, we use the markers in the editor gutter located at the beginning and at the end of the block code in the source file. This is shown in the figure given below:

```
public boolean onCreateOptionsMenu(Menu menu) {

    // Inflate the menu; this adds items to the action bar if it is present.
    getMenuInflater().inflate(R.menu.android_sample, menu);
    return true;
```

Once you click on either of the above markers, the statement will be folded in such a way that only the line with the signature will be left visible.

```
⊞    public boolean onCreateOptionsMenu(Menu menu) {...}
```

If you need to unfoldg some code which has been collapsed, you just have to click on the "+" symbol and you will have your code back. Sometimes, you might also need to view the code which has been collapsed without having to unfold it. In such a case, you just have to hover the mouse pointer over the {...} and the code will be shown to you. This collapsed code will be shown in a lens overlay.

The key sequences for Ctrl-Shift-Plus and Ctrl-Shift-Minus can be used for the purpose of folding and unfolding a piece of code contained in a file.

Also, it is good for you to know that once the Android Studio's code editor has a file opened inside, it will display some sections of the file in a folded manner by default. If you need

to change how this is done, you have to navigate through "File

-> Settings..." and then choose "Editor -> General -> Code

Folding" in the settings panel which is launched.

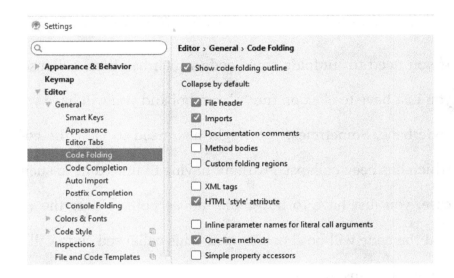

Quick Documentation Lookup

Java and Android documentations which are context sensitive can be accessed once we place the cursor over our declaration over which the declaration is needed and then pressing the keyboard shortcut of Ctrl-Q. With that, a popup having the necessary reference documentation will be displayed. Consider the figure given below which shows the documentation for Android menu class:

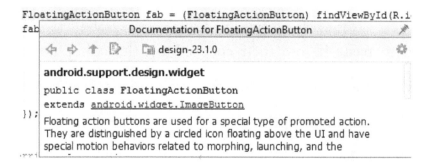

Once the documentation popup has been displayed, we can move it around the screen as shown. Once you click on the push pin icon which is located at the right hand corner of your popup title bar, it will ensure your popup remains visible once the focus has moved back to the editor, and the documentation will be left visible as a reference when we are typing our code.

Code Reformatting

The default setting is that the code editor in Android Studio will format one's code in terms of spacing, indenting, and how statements and code blocks are nested as they are being added. In some situations where we need to reformat multiple lines of code, which is very common especially when one has copied a piece of code from a particular web page and they need to paste it into their code editor, the editor normally provides the user with a tool for editing the source code and once this tool has been selected, it will reformat the code so that it matches how the prevailing code style should be.

For us to reformat our source code, we have to reformat the keyboard shortcut sequence of Ctrl-Alt-L. For the reformat code dialog to be displayed, just press the keys Ctrl-Alt-Shift-L. With that option, you will be in a position to edit only the source code which has been currently selected, the entire file with source code which is active in the editor at the current, or maybe the code which had changed because of an update on the source code control. The figure given below shows what the dialog looks like:

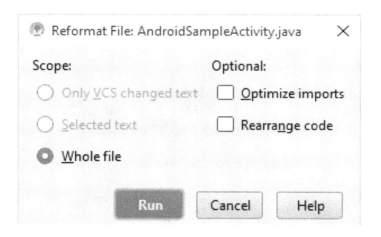

The full range of our source code preferences is changeable via the setting dialog for our project. Select the menu option for *"File -> Settings"* and then select the code style from the panel on the left hand side, and you will be in a position to access the list of programming and markup languages which are supported. Once you have selected a particular language, you will be presented with a wide variety of options on how you can format your code, and these are modifiable via the default of Android Studio so as to match the code style which you prefer. If you need to change the settings configuration for the option Rearrange code in the dialog given above, like unfolding the code style section, just select the Java, and from your Java settings, just select the Arrangement tab.

To conclude about the code editor in Android Studio, it reduces the amount of typing that you need when writing your code and at the same time, it makes it easy for you to navigate through the code and makes it easy for you to read it. This means that the app development process is made much easier for the programmer.

Chapter 2- The Designer Tool in Android Studio

It will be impossible for anyone to think of an Android app which has no user interface. In most Android devices, the users are provided with a touch screen which enables them to interact with the Android apps installed on their devices. Typically, for such interactions to take place, a user interface has to be provided to the user.

For any Android app to be liked by its users, it has to be easy for them to use. As an Android developer, it is good for you to come up with a user interface which is highly interactive and easy to use on the part of users. However, depending on the design requirements of the app, the developer has to stick to these, and the resulting interface can be simple or complex. With the Designer Tool in Android Studio, the process of designing, creating, and implementing user interfaces in Android apps is made much simpler.

Empty vs. Blank Activity Templates

As you are aware, there are numerous activities in an Android application. An activity just represents a standalone module in an Android app and this will directly correlate to a single screen of a user interface. This means that whenever one is working with the Designer Tool, we are after making the layout of our activity.

Whenever we are creating a new project in Android Studio, we will have a number of templates which we can use as the user interface for our activity. The basic templates for these are the Blank Activity and Empty Activity. Most people usually see these as being the same, but they are different from each other. You learn these and you get used to using them when making the interface for your apps.

With the Empty Activity templates, a single layout file will be created, and this will have an instance of RelativeLayout manager with a TextView object.

With the Blank Activity, we will have two layout files. The top level one will have a CoordinatorLayout working as the root view, a menu which has been preconfigured using a single menu item, a configurable app bar, a reference to your second layout file, and a floating action button.

The Empty Activity template will be very useful when we don't need a floating point button or a menu in the activity and there is no need for a special app bar behavior which has been provided by the CoordinatorLayout like options for making the app bar and the toolbar to collapse from being viewed when certain scrolling operations are being done. The Blank Activity is also useful when it comes to provision of the above elements by default. It is always easier for you to use the Blank Activity template for creation of an activity and then delete the elements which are not needed than having to use the Empty

Activity Template. With that, the rest of the functionalities such as collapsing of toolbars and floating action button can be implemented later.

In case you need a menu rather than a floating action button, just make use of the Blank Activity template and then delete the float action button by following the steps given below:

Double-click on your main activity layout file which is located in the tool window for your project under app -> res -> layout so as to load it to the designer. This should be the layout file which has been prefixed with the "*activity_*" but not the content file which has been prefixed with "*content_*"

Once the layout has been loaded into the designer tool, just select the floating action button, and then tap the Delete key of the keyboard so as to remove the object from the layout.

Locate the Java code and then edit it for the activity, and this can be found in app -> java -> <package name> -> <activity

class name>. Remove the code for the floating action button from the onCreate method as shown below:

@Override

protected void onCreate(Bundle savedInstanceState) {

    super.onCreate(savedInstanceState);

    setContentView(R.layout.activity_main);

    Toolbar   toolbar   =   (Toolbar) findViewById(R.id.toolbar);

    setSupportActionBar(toolbar);

}

If you need the the floating action button rather than the menu, make use of the Blank Activity template and follow the steps which are given below:

Edit the class file for your activity, and then delete the methods "*onOptionsItemSelected*" and "*onCreateOptionsMenu.*"

Choose the res -> menu item in the tool window for your project, and then hit the Delete key on your keyboard so as to remove the folder and the associated resource files from your project.

Android Studio Designer

The Designer tool in Android Studio provides us with an environment in the form of "what you see is what you get" (WYSIWYG). In this type of environment, we are expected to select views from a palette, which should then be placed onto a canvas which is how they appear on a real Android device. Once we have placed our view onto the canvas, it is possible for us to resize it, move it, or even delete the view. The properties panel can be used for the purpose of modifying the properties associated with the view which you have selected.

What happens is that the Designer tool just constructs the XML file for the user interface of your Android app. This is why the designer tool has to operate in two modes, mainly the Text mode and the Designer mode.

Designer Mode

In this type of mode, one can visually modify the user interface via a direct usage of view palette and graphical representation of the layout.

Consider the figure given below, which shows the Android Designer tool already in design mode:

The following is an explanation of the various parts of the Android designer tool when in the design mode:

1. Palette- this will provide us with access to the wide range of the view components which the Android SDK provides. To make it easy for navigation, these have been grouped into categories. If you need to add any component to the layout, you can drag it from the palette into the best position in the layout you wish or by just clicking on the necessary component on the palette and then clicking on the position it is to be placed in the layout.

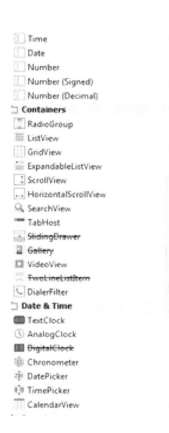

Time
Date
Number
Number (Signed)
Number (Decimal)
Containers
RadioGroup
ListView
GridView
ExpandableListView
ScrollView
HorizontalScrollView
SearchView
TabHost
SlidingDrawer
Gallery
VideoView
TwoLineListItem
DialerFilter
Date & Time
TextClock
AnalogClock
DigitalClock
Chronometer
DatePicker
TimePicker
CalendarView

2. Device Screen

This is the part which will provide you with a visual view of the interface as it is being designed. This layout will allow for a direct manipulation of our design when we are in need of selecting, deleting, moving, and resizing the screen elements. For us to change the design model of the layout which has been presented, we can use the menu which is located in the toolbar to do this at any time.

Sometimes, you may find the image of the frame which is surrounding the display to be distracting. However, it is possible for you to turn this one off by selecting the settings menu from the toolbar represented with a gear icon and then toggling the option for "Include Device Frames if you find it.

3. Component Tree

As you are aware, for us to construct a user interface for an Android app, we have to use a hierarchical structure. With the component tree, we are provided with a visual overview of how our user interface has been designed. Once you have selected an element in the component tree, you will observe that its corresponding view in the layout will be selected. Similarly, once you have selected a view on the layout of the device screen, the view will also be selected in the component tree hierarchy.

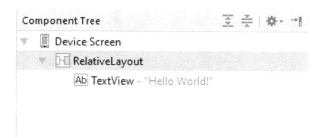

4. Properties

All the component views which have been listed in the palette are associated with some properties which can be used for the purpose of adjusting the look and behavior of those components. The property panel of the Designer will provide us with access to properties of the view which has currently been selected in the layout, and this will allow for changes to be made.

Properties   ? ↩ ▼

layout:width	match_parent
layout:height	match_parent
style	
accessibilityLiveRegion	
accessibilityTraversalAfte	

5. Toolbar

The toolbar in the Designer will provide us with access to a variety of options such as the ability to zoom the screen of the device in and out, the ability to change the design model which has currently been displayed, change the layout to either portrait or landscape to a different level of the Android SDK. The toolbar will also provide you with a set of buttons which are context-sensitive which always appear after selection of the relevant view types in the layout of the device screen.

Palette   ❖· ↑ ⬚· ▤ Nexus 4· ⬚· ⓘ AppTheme ▢MainActivity· ⓘ· 📱23·   Component Tree   ⊞ ⊟ ❖· ↑

6. Mode Switching Tabs

These tans are located along the lower edge of your designer, and they provide us with a mechanism on how to switch between the Text and the design mode of the Designer tool.

Text Mode

You have to note that the Designer tool in Android Studio lets users create the user interface part of their apps in an easy manner. This is done in the XML resource layout file. You can view and edit the XML layout file at any time that you want during the development process by clicking on the Text tab which can be found in the bottom Panel of the Designer tool. For you to return to the design mode, you just have to click on the Designer tab.

The following are the various parts of the Android Designer Tool when viewed in text mode:

1. Editor- this part of the designer tool is used for displaying the XML part of the current interface layout design. An example of this part is shown in the figure given below:

```xml
<?xml version="1.0" encoding="utf-8"?>
<RelativeLayout xmlns:android="http://schemas.android.com/apk/res/a
    xmlns:tools="http://schemas.android.com/tools" android:layout_w
    android:layout_height="match_parent" android:paddingLeft="16dp"
    android:paddingRight="16dp"
    android:paddingTop="16dp"
    android:paddingBottom="16dp" tools:context=".MainActivity">

    <TextView android:text="Hello World!" android:layout_width="wra
        android:layout_height="wrap_content" />
</RelativeLayout>
```

The code can be edited or deleted from the editor.

2. Preview- as you are making changes to the code which is contained in the editor, the changes which are applied will be previewed in this window. The changes are reflected immediately on the preview window as they are made on the XML code, meaning that we will not need to change between the text and design mode for them to see the changes made. The preview will not allow us to manipulate our code directly, but once we have double clicked on the view in the preview, it will help us switch to the preview mode and then preselect the corresponding view in the layout of device screen.

Hello World!

3. Toolbar- the toolbar in the text mode will provide us with a subset of the functions which are available in the design mode with an additional button for taking a screenshot of the screen layout which is currently active. Below is a figure showing the toolbar:

4. Mode Switching Tabs- these are the tabs which are located along the lower edge of your Designer, and these provide us with a mechanism on how to switch between the Text and the Designer modes.

Setting Properties

The panel for properties provides us with access to all of the settings which are available for the component which is currently selected. Once you click on the panel and then begin to type some characters, then the closest match of what you type will be shown to you. However, despite the fact that the properties for the component are displayed in the properties panel, we can access these properties quickly by double-clicking on the component view which is located in the layout. Once you double-click on a TextView component, you are given a quick access to the text and even the ID of your view. You will then be in a position to edit these and save on time.

In the case of some properties located both in the quick access view and the main properties window they have three dots, which are usually located on a button. For properties having a finite number of options, one will be provided with a drop-down menu having these. In the latter case, it is just an indication that you will be presented with a settings dialog which will help you select the right property according to what you need.

By default, only the properties which are mostly listed will be displayed in the properties panel. If you need to access the full range of properties for the component which you have currently selected, just switch your panel into the expert mode. To toggle this on and off, you just have to click on the funnel button which is located on the toolbar.

In most cases, you will not need to access the expert mode properties. However, it will be good for you to know more about this, as you may not find the property that you need in the standard mode.

Type Morphing

With the type morphing feature in the Designer tool of Android Studio, a component view which is already part of our user interface can be changed from one type to another. A good example of this is when you have a TextView. This can easily be changed to an EditText by use of the Type morphing feature. However, you have to note that morphing is limited to the types of conversions which can be done in Android Studio. For example, it is impossible for one to convert an EditText into a ProgressBar. Also, you have to note that this feature does not provide us with a quicker alternative on how we can delete components and then add new ones.

If you need to morph a particular component, just right-click on its corresponding view in the layout and then menu option for Morphing, and this should be followed by the type to which the view is to be changed. In the figure given below, the available options for morphing in a ImageButton are shown:

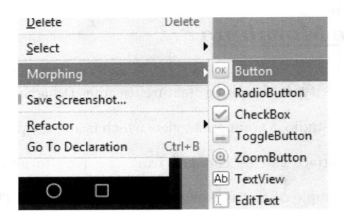

The ImageButton can be morphed into any of the above elements or components.

Creation of a Custom Device Definition

The device menu of our Designer toolbar provides us with the device types which have been preconfigured, and once these have been selected, they will be shown as the canvas of our device screen. Other than the types of devices which have been preconfigured, any instance of the AVD which had been previously configured in the Android Studio environment will also be shown within the menu. For additional device configurations to be added, and display the device menu, just select the option for "Add Device Definition..." and then follow the steps which are necessary for setting an AVD (Android Virtual Device).

Chapter 3- Designing the User Interface with Android Designer

The Designer Tool in Android Studio is the easiest mechanism by which one can design and create a user interface for their Android apps.

For you to do this you have to begin by creating the project for your Android app. Launch the Android Studio and then close any projects which might be open. You can then follow the necessary steps so as to create a new Android project.

Creation of a New Activity

Once the project has been created, you should create a new activity. Press the Alt-1 keyboard shortcut so as to display the tool window for your project. Once this has been displayed, just unfold the hierarchy by clicking on the arrows facing the right next to the entries located on the project window. Once the package name for your project becomes visible, just right-click on it and then choose the menu options for New -> Activity -> Empty Activity menu.

In the new activity dialog which appears, just give the activity a name and the layout. As you are aware, your activity will always expect a layout resource file, so make sure that the option for this is enabled. This should be the option "Generate Layout File." For your app to be in a position to run on the device, we have to create an activity and designate it as the "*Launcher*" activity. If you do not implement this, then the operating system will fail to know the app which it should launch once it has been started. This will mean that the activity will not be started. Note that in our case, we have only one activity, so we have to designate this as the launcher activity.

At this point, two files should have been added to the project. Note that we chose the Empty Activity template for our activity, so our layout file should be located in activity_layout_sample.xml, and we should have no other content layout file.

Finally, you have to add the activity file which you have just created into the file AndroidManifest.xml, and then designated to be the launcher activity. The manifest file for your project can be found in the folder "app -> manifests" and this should have the XML code given below:

```
<?xml version="1.0" encoding="utf-8"?>

<manifest
xmlns:android=http://schemas.android.com/apk/res/android

    package="com.myproject.layoutfile" >


    <application

        android:allowBackup="true"

        android:icon="@mipmap/ic_launcher"

        android:label="@string/app_name"

        android:supportsRtl="true"

        android:theme="@style/AppTheme" >
```

```xml
<activity android:name=".LayoutFileActivity" >

    <intent-filter>

        <action
android:name="android.intent.action.MAIN" />

        <category
android:name="android.intent.category.LAUNCHER" />

    </intent-filter>

</activity>

</application>

</manifest>
```

How to Design the User Interface

Locate the layout file "activity_layout_sample.xml" and then double-click on it. This can be found in the folder "app -> res -> layout" and the file will be loaded into the designer tool. The default setting is that the component should have a single component in the form of a Text View which will display the text "Hello World!" You can delete this component by selecting it and then pressing the delete key on your keyboard.

From the category for the widgets, just drag a button view object into the center of the layout. The green horizontal and vertical lines will appear so as to show the location of the component on the layout. Just center the component onto the layout, and then release the mouse to drop it there. Click on a plain text object, and then drag it from the section from the Text fields section of the palette, and then drag and drop it at a position relatively above the component we previously dragged.

Click on your light bulb icon so as to display the hints menu, and then click on the message labeled ""This text field does not specify an inputType or a hint." In the dialog for Set Attribute Value, select Text as the input type. Dismiss the dialog by clicking on the Ok button, and then set the attribute.

How to Edit the View Properties

Once you have placed your view object into the layout, one can edit the properties of that component from the Designer tool. Of course, the width of the EditText may not be large enough to allow the user to type the text that they need. For you to enlarge the width, just select the EditText component and then locate the width property from the property panel. A field for value will be provided, so just enter the right value for the width according to the size that you need. The value that you enter should be in the following list of units of measurements:

- in – Inches.

- mm – Millimeters.

- pt – Points (1/72 of an inch).

- dp – Density-independent pixels. This is an abstract unit of measurement based on the physical density of your device display relative to the 160dpi display baseline.

- sp – Scale-independent pixels. Similar to dp, but scaled based on the user's font preference.

- px – The actual screen pixels. Its use is not recommended, since the different screens will have different pixels per inch. It is good for you to use dp in preference to this unit.

You can then double-click on the button, and then edit the text which appears on it. You can then click on your light bulb icon which has been displayed and then the I18N message so as to display the dialog for the Extract Resource. Just give it a name and then click on the Ok button so as to create a string resource for the button.

You now have a complete simple user interface for your Android app. If you need to design a complex user interface for your Android app, you just have to follow the steps given above, but you can drag and drop any components that you need from the palette. Once you have dropped the components into the layout, just change their properties the way you need, and nest the layouts according to your need and you have an amazing user interface for you Android app.

At this point, you can run the app so as to perform testing. Identify the Run button from the toolbar of the main window, and then click on it so as to run the app. Select to run the app either on the emulator or on a real Android device, and then wait for the app to be opened. If there are no errors in your app, then you will see it displayed on the emulator or the real device as you have selected, and the user interface will appear as you designed it in the designer tool of the Android Studio.

Creating the XML Layout Manually

As you might have noticed, it is easy for one to create the user interface for the ir Android app by use of the designer tool, and their productivity will be improved. However, it is still possible for us to edit the XML file manually so as to create the interface. As you might have noted, once you drag and drop the components on the layout, the XML code is generated automatically, meaning that you may not be expected to know much about the code. However, in this section, we will show you how to edit the code manually and get the user interface that you desire to have.

The following line of code, which is a declaration, should form the first line of any XML file in Android:

<?xml version="1.0" encoding="utf-8"?>

The above declaration should then be followed by the root element of your layout, which is the container view like the layout manager. This is usually represented by opening and closing tags, and the rest of properties which one needs to set on the view.

Consider the XML file given below in which the Relative Layout has been set as the root element while match parent has been set so as to fill up all of the available space on the parent. Here is the code for the XML:

<RelativeLayout

xmlns:android=http://schemas.android.com/apk/res /android

    xmlns:tools="http://schemas.android.com/tools"

    android:layout_width="match_parent"

    android:layout_height="match_parent"

    android:paddingLeft="16dp"

    android:paddingRight="16dp"

    android:paddingTop="16dp"

android:paddingBottom="16dp"

tools:context="com.myproject.layoutfile.LayoutFileA ctivity">

</RelativeLayout>

For any child element which is nested into the Relative Layout, it has been to be included within the opening and the closing tags. Consider the XML file given below in which we have added a button and edittext as the child of the RelativeLayout:

<RelativeLayout

xmlns:android=http://schemas.android.com/apk/res /android

xmlns:tools="http://schemas.android.com/tools"

android:layout_width="match_parent"

android:layout_height="match_parent"

android:paddingLeft="16dp"

android:paddingRight="16dp"

android:paddingTop="16dp"

```
    android:paddingBottom="16dp"

tools:context="com.myproject.layoutfile.LayoutFileA
ctivity">

    <Button

        android:layout_width="wrap_content"

        android:layout_height="wrap_content"

        android:text="@string/button_string"

        android:id="@+id/button"

        android:layout_centerVertical="true"

        android:layout_centerHorizontal="true" />


    <EditText

        android:layout_width="wrap_content"

        android:layout_height="wrap_content"

        android:id="@+id/editText"

        android:layout_above="@+id/button"

        android:layout_centerHorizontal="true"

        android:layout_marginBottom="56dp"

        android:inputType="text"
```

android:width="350dp" />

</RelativeLayout>

You should note that our two child components have some properties declared within them. The button itself has an id and the text which it is to display to the user. The button has also been centered vertically and horizontally within the parent view, and the its width and height set to wrap content so that they can fit well on the display of the device. The content will also be well accommodated.

The width of the Edit Text has also been set, and this has been centered horizontally. With that, you will have a complete user interface which you have created manually rather than by using the designer tool. However, the matter of the method to use to create the user interface will depend on your preference. However, there are some advantages which one enjoys once they use the designer tool so as to create the user interface.

Of course, with the designer tool, you are not expected to type any XML code, and this makes it faster for you to create your user interface. With the design mode, you are not expected to learn much about the design classes of the Android SDK view classes.

However, despite the fact that we have discussed the two ways to use these two mechanisms when creating the user interface for our apps, the two methods are in no way mutually exclusive. In most cases, people create the user interface by use of the design mode, but whenever they need to make some modifications or changes to the user interface, they directly edit the code.

Use of the Hierarchy Viewer

The hierarchy viewer is a very important tool for the purpose of inspection of the view hierarchy of an activity. The tool is commonly used for the purpose of providing a detailed view of the whole view tree for the activities which are within the applications which are currently running and then provide some insight into the layout which is currently rendering the performance.

The hierarchy viewer can only be used for inspection of the apps which are only running within the emulator, or a device which is running a development version of Android.

If you need to use this tool for the Layout Sample app which we have just created, just launch the app on the emulator device and wait until you see the app displayed on the emulator. At the time when it is running, just select the menu option Tools -> Android -> Android Device Monitor. From your DDMS window, just select the Window -> Open

Perspective... and then select the Hierarchy view from the dialog which results and then click on the Ok button.

Once the Hierarchy viewer has appeared, it will be made up of a number of different panels. The left hand window will list all the windows which are currently active on the emulator such as the status bar, the launcher, and the navigation bar.

Chapter 4- Use of Java Code in Android 6 to Create the User Interface

You should now be aware of how to create the user interface of your Android app by use of the Designer tool, either in text or design mode. Also, one can use the Java code so as to create the user interface for your app. This will be discussed in this chapter, and you get to know both the advantages and the disadvantages of using this approach.

To demonstrate how this can be done in Android design, just begin by creating an Android project after launching the Android Studio. You should also ensure that you have created a Java activity named "JavaLayoutActivity" and its associated layout activity named "activity java layout." The Java file will be automatically loaded into the code editor.

To add the views to the activity, just begin by performing a deletion of the following code:

```
@Override
protected void onCreate(Bundle savedInstanceState)
{
        super.onCreate(savedInstanceState);
}
```

The next step should involve addition of a RelativeLayout to our code, having a single button as the child view. New instances of the RelativeLayout and the Button classes should be created and then added to the activity. The button view should be added to the RelativeLayout as a child which should then be displayed by use of the method "setContentView()." The following code best demonstrates how this can be done:

```
package com.myproject.javalayout;
import android.widget.Button;
import android.support.v7.app.AppCompatActivity;
```

```java
import android.widget.RelativeLayout;

import android.os.Bundle;


public class JavaLayoutActivity extends
AppCompatActivity {

    @Override

    protected void onCreate(Bundle
savedInstanceState) {

        super.onCreate(savedInstanceState);

        Button btn = new Button(this);

        RelativeLayout myLayout = new
RelativeLayout(this);

        myLayout.addView(btn);

        setContentView(myLayout);

    }

}

.

.

.

}
```

The necessary properties should also be added to the components. We need to make the background of the RelativeLayout blue and our Button to display the text *"Click Me"* to the user on a green background. The Java code can then be modified to the following so that we can achieve those properties:

package com.myproject.javalayout;

import android.support.v7.app.AppCompatActivity;

import android.widget.Button;

import android.os.Bundle;

import android.graphics.Color;

import android.widget.RelativeLayout;

public class JavaLayoutActivity extends AppCompatActivity {

   @Override

   protected void onCreate(Bundle savedInstanceState) {

     super.onCreate(savedInstanceState);

```
Button btn = new Button(this);

btn.setText("Click Me");

btn.setBackgroundColor(Color.GREEN);


RelativeLayout myLayout = new
RelativeLayout(this);

myLayout.setBackgroundColor(Color.BLUE);


myLayout.addView(btn);

setContentView(myLayout);
  }
.

.

.

}
```

Once you compile and then run the app at this time, the interface will be displayed in the way we have designed it. The background will be blue, while button will display the text *"Click Me"* on a green background.

The layout parameters can be set by use of the code given below:

RelativeLayout.LayoutParams buttonParams =

new RelativeLayout.LayoutParams(

RelativeLayout.LayoutParams.WRAP_CONTENT,

RelativeLayout.LayoutParams.WRAP_CONTENT);

The above code will create the LayoutParams object for our button. With that setting, both the width and the height of the button will only be large enough to accommodate the text *"Click Me."* We should then add some rules which will help us center the button vertically and horizontally. This can be done with the code given below:

buttonParams.addRule(RelativeLayout.CENTER_HO RIZONTAL);

buttonParams.addRule(RelativeLayout.CENTER_VE RTICAL);

Conclusion

We have come to the conclusion of this guide. Android Studio 6 has brought in numerous features which Android software developers can take advantage of to improve their productivity and deliver better apps. It is now easy for you to design the user interface by use of the Designer tool in Android Studio.

This tool can be used in either text or design mode. When in design mode, you just have to drag the components from the palette, and then drop them into the layout. The properties of the component can then be adjusted to what one wants.

This process is very easy, and one creates the user interface in a fast manner. When in text mode, one has to use the XML coding so as to create the user interface. This is a bit slow compared to using the design mode.

However, the kind of method to use should depend on one's choice, as some people prefer the design mode while others like the text mode.

It is also possible to create the user interface for our Android app using the Java code, and purely Java code, without having to worry about the XML code. This has been discussed.

www.ingramcontent.com/pod-product-compliance
Lightning Source LLC
Chambersburg PA
CBHW061030050326
40689CB00012B/2754